r   E

D1716923

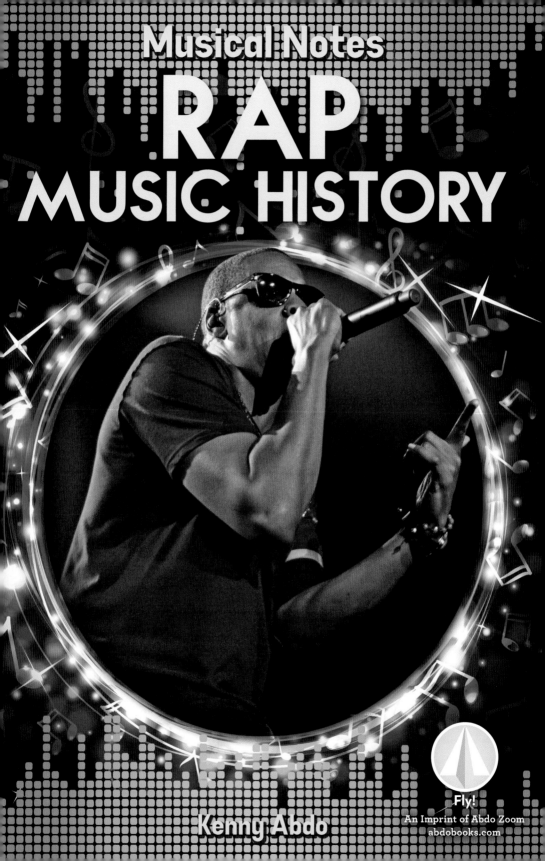

Musical Notes
RAP
MUSIC HISTORY

Kenny Abdo

Fly!
An Imprint of Abdo Zoom
abdobooks.com

abdobooks.com

Published by Abdo Zoom, a division of ABDO, P.O. Box 398166, Minneapolis, Minnesota 55439. Copyright © 2020 by Abdo Consulting Group, Inc. International copyrights reserved in all countries. No part of this book may be reproduced in any form without written permission from the publisher. Fly!™ is a trademark and logo of Abdo Zoom.

Printed in the United States of America, North Mankato, Minnesota.
102019
012020

Photo Credits: Alamy, AP Images, Everett Collection, Shutterstock
Production Contributors: Kenny Abdo, Jennie Forsberg, Grace Hansen
Design Contributors: Dorothy Toth, Neil Klinepier

Library of Congress Control Number: 2019941322

Publisher's Cataloging-in-Publication Data

Names: Abdo, Kenny, author.
Title: Rap music history / by Kenny Abdo
Description: Minneapolis, Minnesota : Abdo Zoom, 2020 | Series: Musical notes |
    Includes online resources and index.
Identifiers: ISBN 9781532129445 (lib. bdg.) | ISBN 9781098220426 (ebook) |
    ISBN 9781098220914 (Read-to-Me ebook)
Subjects: LCSH: Rap (Music)--Juvenile literature. | Music and history--Juvenile
    literature. | Rap (Music)--History and criticism--Juvenile literature. | Gangsta rap
    (Music)--Juvenile literature. | Rap (Music)--Social aspects--Juvenile literature.
Classification: DDC 782.421649--dc23

TABLE OF CONTENTS

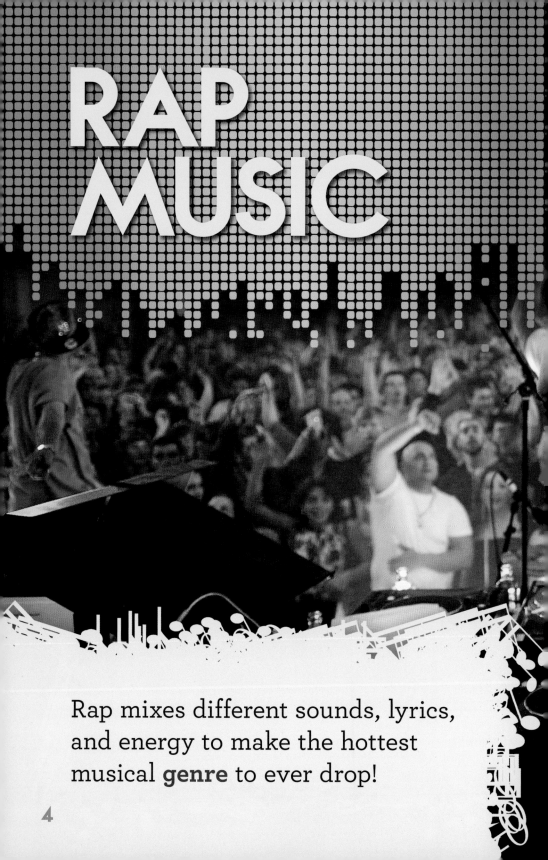

RAP MUSIC

Rap mixes different sounds, lyrics, and energy to make the hottest musical **genre** to ever drop!

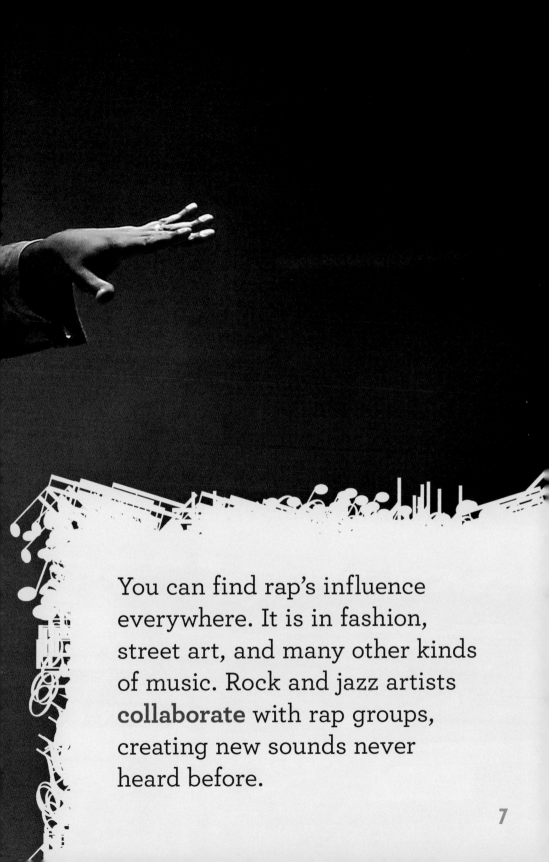

You can find rap's influence everywhere. It is in fashion, street art, and many other kinds of music. Rock and jazz artists **collaborate** with rap groups, creating new sounds never heard before.

OPENING ACT

At a birthday party in 1973 in the Bronx, New York, DJ Kool Herc used two **turntables** to mix two songs together. Many believe this was the birth of rap and hip-hop.

In 1979, Sugar Hill Gang released "Rapper's Delight." **Sampling** the disco song "Good Times" by Chic, it was an overnight success. The **single** brought rap to the forefront of popular music.

HEADLINER

Run-DMC was the first rap group to appear on **MTV** in the 80s. The group's mix of humor and honesty scored them gold, platinum, and multiplatinum records. It was a first for a rap group.

Rappers began experimenting with other musicians and sounds in the mid-80s. The Beastie Boys started as a punk band. Then in 1986, they released *Licensed to Ill*. Their wild rhymes, beats, and energy opened new doors to make rap truly unique.

By the 90s, rap had split into west and east coast groups. Tupac Shakur and Dr. Dre rapped about the sunbaked antics of California.

A Tribe Called Quest and The Notorious B.I.G. told tales about NYC, the city that never sleeps.

Jay-Z, Eminem, and Kanye West turned rap into a lifestyle. Jay-Z became a **label** president, head of a clothing line, and record breaker. He has the most #1 albums of any solo artist in history.

Lil Nas X's **single**, "Old Town Road," made history in 2019. The song was on the top of the Billboard Hot 100 list for an amazing 17 weeks! The hit tune proves that rap will keep on spinning long into the future.

GLOSSARY

collaborate – to work with another person or group in order to do something or reach a goal.

genre – a type of art, music, or literature.

label – the branded company that markets and releases music.

Music Television (MTV) – an international cable television channel that debuted in 1981. It was a first of its kind to play new and popular music videos around the clock.

sampling – reusing a part of a song in another song.

single – an individual song from a full album released as promotion.

turntable – a rotating stand with a magnetic cartridge that plays musical records.

ONLINE RESOURCES

Booklinks
NONFICTION NETWORK
FREE! ONLINE NONFICTION RESOURCES

To learn more about
rap music history, please visit
abdobooklinks.com or scan
this QR code. These links
are routinely monitored and
updated to provide the most
current information available.

INDEX